GOD IS PRETTY GOOD AT SECOND CHANCES

STUDY GUIDE

Published by Dream Releaser Publishing

Cover design by Sara Young
Cover photo by James Robinson

ISBN: 978-1-962401-31-9   1 2 3 4 5 6 7 8 9 10

Printed in the United States of America

GOD IS PRETTY GOOD AT SECOND CHANCES

MY PERSONAL STORY

RAQUEL COPELAND

STUDY GUIDE

DREAM RELEASER PUBLISHING

CONTENTS

GOD IS PRETTY GOOD AT SECOND CHANCES

MY
PERSONAL
STORY

RAQUEL COPELAND

CHAPTER 1

MOTHERLESS: TRIUMPH OVER TRAUMA

Embrace the sadness and hurt or embrace the redeeming God who will be what you need at every moment in your life.

REFLECT AND TAKE ACTION:

In what area(s) of your life have you felt deprived of something important to you?

_____

_____

_____

_____

_____

_____

_____

_____

_____

_____

In your own words, what do you think is the need underlying the void you felt?

_____

_____

_____

_____

_____

_____

_____

_____

_____

_____

_____

_____

In what ways has God met that need, even if in a different way than what you would desire or expect?

_____

_____

_____

_____

_____

_____

_____

_____

_____

Where are you in your healing process? Where are the wounds that still need healing?

_____

_____

_____

_____

_____

_____

_____

_____

_____

Where have you seen God's love and care show up for you following a loss?

_____

_____

_____

_____

_____

_____

_____

_____

_____

Do you feel like you have let God into those places in your heart that are hurting? How can you begin to invite Him to bind up your wounds?

_____

_____

_____

_____

_____

_____

_____

_____

_____

CHAPTER 2

A TWENTY-YEAR JOURNEY FOR A FOUR-YEAR DEGREE

*I chose my faith and put myself
in position to allow the anointing
of God to reconnect me,
restore me, and revive me.*

REFLECT AND TAKE ACTION:

Reflecting back on your life up to this point, in what areas has God surprised you with His plans for your life?

_____

_____

_____

_____

_____

_____

_____

_____

_____

_____

What was it like for your expectations to be infringed upon? How did that feel and how has that feeling changed for you?

_____

_____

_____

_____

_____

_____

_____

_____

_____

Consider the scripture above and answer the following questions:

What do you think this scripture says about God's sovereignty and power?

_____

_____

_____

_____

_____

_____

_____

_____

_____

How do you think this applies to your own story, perhaps in times when God has asked you to take a sharp left turn that you didn't plan for or expect?

_____

_____

_____

_____

_____

_____

_____

_____

_____

_____

_____

In what ways does this promise provide comfort to you?

_____

_____

_____

_____

_____

_____

_____

_____

_____

_____

_____

Can you identify a time in your life when you looked back and understood why God had you change course?

_____

_____

_____

_____

_____

_____

_____

_____

_____

_____

What has God deposited within you that may be an indicator of His plan for your life? Are you confident that the path you're traveling on is where He wants you?

_____

_____

_____

_____

_____

_____

_____

_____

_____

_____

What questions are you wrestling with about where God wants to use your gifts and talents?

_____

_____

_____

_____

_____

_____

_____

_____

_____

_____

PAYCHECK OR PURPOSE

I'm almost positive had I developed a relationship with God years ago, my eyes would have been opened to my purpose.

As you read Chapter 3: "Paycheck or Purpose" in *God is Pretty Good at Second Chances*, reflect on, and respond to the text by answering the following questions.

REFLECT AND TAKE ACTION:

Where do your greatest passions lie? What gets you up in the morning and makes your heart skip a beat?

_____

_____

_____

_____

_____

_____

_____

_____

_____

_____

How closely are you fulfilling and living out those passions? Why or why not?

_____

_____

_____

_____

_____

_____

_____

_____

_____

_____

> "For I know the plans I have for you," declares
> the LORD, "plans to prosper you and not to harm
> you, plans to give you hope and a future."
>
> —Jeremiah 29:11 (NIV)

*Consider the scripture above and answer the following
questions:*

How does this scripture challenge the fears or reservations
you have about your future?

_____

_____

_____

_____

_____

_____

_____

_____

_____

Why do you think that what sometimes appears harmful is
actually God's gesture of His mercy and grace over your life?

_____

_____

_____

_____

_____

_____

_____

_____

_____

_____

_____

In your own words, what do you think Jeremiah means by the word "prosper?" What does prospering entail? What does it not entail?

_____

_____

_____

_____

_____

_____

_____

_____

_____

What does the author's story about her gradual promotions in her career tell you about God's promise to reward those who devote their work to the Lord and to serve others?

_____

_____

_____

_____

_____

_____

_____

_____

_____

Has God ever called you to something that you felt completely underqualified for? In what ways did He set you up for success?

_____

_____

_____

_____

_____

_____

_____

_____

_____

Where have you seen God's unending patience in your life?
What was your big "second chance?"

_____

_____

_____

_____

_____

_____

_____

_____

_____

_____

THE CALL AND THE RESPONSE

I continued to serve, and I found myself yearning for God more and more. I wanted to read more, study more, and just be in God's presence.

As you read
Chapter 4:
"The Call and
the Response"
in *God is Pretty
Good at Second
Chances*,
reflect on,
and respond
to the text
by answering
the following
questions.

REFLECT AND TAKE ACTION:

Why do you think pouring yourself into service produces a greater hunger for the Word and presence of God?

_____

_____

_____

_____

_____

_____

_____

_____

_____

_____

The author refers to her lack of awareness of what God wanted her to do as "the unknowing." What do you do in the "unknowing" places in your life? Does it work?

_____

_____

_____

_____

_____

_____

_____

_____

_____

_____

> "Let us not become weary in doing good, for at the
> proper time we will reap a harvest if we do not give up.
>
> —Galatians 6:9 (NIV)

*Consider the scripture above and answer the following
questions:*

What does or has "doing good" looked like in your life in
accordance with the places God has assigned you to serve?
Where is your ministry?

_____

_____

_____

_____

_____

_____

_____

_____

_____

Where and when does weariness seem to surface in the work
that you do for the Kingdom? How do you respond to that
weariness?

_____

_____

_____

_____

_____

_____

_____

_____

_____

_____

Think about a time when you felt like giving up or almost
gave up. What kept you going?

_____

_____

_____

_____

_____

_____

_____

_____

_____

Why do you think perseverance is so powerful in times of uncertainty and ambiguity? How might throwing in the towel worsen the frustration of uncertainty?

_____

_____

_____

_____

_____

_____

_____

_____

_____

Where are you needing God's strength to accomplish His mission for your life? Where are you feeling the weakest?

_____

_____

_____

_____

_____

_____

_____

_____

_____

Who is traveling along your journey with you? How is that partnership and fellowship helping you to persevere?

_____

_____

_____

_____

_____

_____

_____

_____

_____

How long are you willing to wait to see God's promises and the good works He has called for you to do come to pass?

_____

_____

_____

_____

_____

_____

_____

_____

_____

DIVORCED BUT NOT DENIED LOVE

If you are considering remarriage, be aware of the stumbling blocks in your past and your present.

READING TIME

As you read Chapter 5: "Divorced but Not Denied Love" in *God is Pretty Good at Second Chances*, reflect on, and respond to the text by answering the following questions.

REFLECT AND TAKE ACTION:

In what areas of your life do you see unresolved pain, trauma, anger, or unforgiveness surface in your relationships?

_____

_____

_____

_____

_____

_____

_____

_____

_____

What kind of coping mechanisms have you used to handle conflict or dissatisfaction in your marriage or other relationships?

_____

_____

_____

_____

_____

_____

_____

_____

> "Forget the former things; do not dwell on
> the past. See I am doing a new thing! Now
> it springs up; do you not perceive it?
>
> —Isaiah 43:18-19 (NIV)

*Consider the scripture above and answer the following
questions:*

Are there things in the past that you find yourself dwelling on
today? Why have they been particularly difficult to move past?

_____

_____

_____

_____

_____

_____

_____

_____

_____

What "new thing" is God doing in your life? What "old
thing" do you need to let go of in order to receive the new?

_____

_____

_____

_____

_____

_____

_____

_____

_____

_____

Are you resisting the new thing God is doing in your life?
Have you resisted them in the past? What do you think is at
the root of that resistance?

_____

_____

_____

_____

_____

_____

_____

_____

_____

What do you think healing from the wounds of your past looks like when you are trying to make a marriage or relationship work?

_____

_____

_____

_____

_____

_____

_____

_____

_____

How can you find success coming into a relationship as a broken person?

_____

_____

_____

_____

_____

_____

_____

_____

_____

What kind of behaviors from your spouse, friends, or loved ones seem to trigger you? How could you view that person through a lens of compassion rather than a burden?

_____

_____

_____

_____

_____

_____

_____

_____

What do you think God may be trying to teach you right now as it pertains to your marriage or other relationships?

_____

_____

_____

_____

_____

_____

_____

_____

_____

BLOOMING: GOD MADE DIRT AND DIRT DON'T HURT

I would argue that when you know who you are and whose you are, transitions may be a bit easier to navigate.

As you read Chapter 6: "Blooming: God Made Dirt and Dirt Don't Hurt" in *God is Pretty Good at Second Chances*, reflect on, and respond to the text by answering the following questions.

REFLECT AND TAKE ACTION:

If you were asked, "Who are you?" how would you respond?

_____

_____

_____

_____

_____

_____

_____

_____

_____

_____

_____

What matters to you? What makes your heart break? How do those core values show up in who you say you are?

_____

_____

_____

_____

_____

_____

_____

_____

_____

_____

_____

> "When Jesus came to the region of Caesarea Philippi, he asked his disciples, 'Who do people say the Son of Man is?'. . . 'But what about you?' he asked. 'Who do you say I am?'"
>
> —Matthew 16:13, 15 (NIV)

Consider the scripture above and answer the following questions:

Who is Jesus to you? What is your relationship with Him like?

_____

_____

_____

_____

_____

_____

_____

_____

_____

_____

Why do you think it is important to know your Savior before you can truly know yourself?

_____

_____

_____

_____

_____

_____

_____

_____

_____

_____

_____

What have you learned about who you are from Him over the past few years?

_____

_____

_____

_____

_____

_____

_____

_____

_____

How do you feel about who you are? What parts bother you? What parts do you feel reflect the heart and character of God the most?

_____

_____

_____

_____

_____

_____

_____

_____

_____

What have you done up until this point to become better acquainted with you? What else do you have to learn?

_____

_____

_____

_____

_____

_____

_____

_____

_____

Refer to the series of questions the author poses in this chapter to help you understand and know yourself more intimately. Are some more difficult to answer than others? Why?

_____

_____

_____

_____

_____

_____

_____

_____

In what ways do you think falling in love with who God created you to be is an act of worship?

_____

_____

_____

_____

_____

_____

_____

_____

_____